This Ladybird ....cture
Book has been specially
planned to illustrate familiar
objects which a child will
enjoy recognizing and
naming. There is just the
right amount of detail in
each one to encourage
comment and conversation
with mother or teacher,
who should talk freely about
the pictures - thus helping
to build up the child's
speech vocabulary. Baby-
talk should always be
avoided.

*The Ladybird Picture Books
are ideally suited for use with
the Ladybird 'Under Five' series—
'Learning with Mother' and its
associated Playbooks.*

A LADYBIRD

First Picture Book

by ETHEL and HARRY WINGFIELD

Publishers: Ladybird Books Ltd . Loughborough
© Ladybird Books Ltd (formerly Wills & Hepworth Ltd) 1970
Printed in England

teddy

Talking about Teddy:

Teddy bears are soft and cuddly. Shall we pretend
to cuddle a Teddy bear?
This Teddy is wearing a blue ribbon.

0 7214 0251 8

shoe

Talking about a shoe:

What a lovely red shoe! What colour are your shoes?
Do your shoes have straps and buckles, or do they have laces?

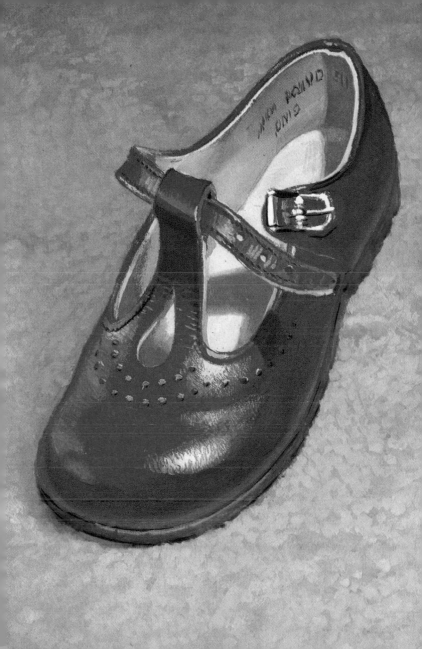

sweets

Talking about sweets:

There are many different coloured sweets in the picture.

Can you see any sweets that are the same colour?

bath

Talking about a bath:

I wonder who will be getting into this bath?
What can you see in the bath tray?

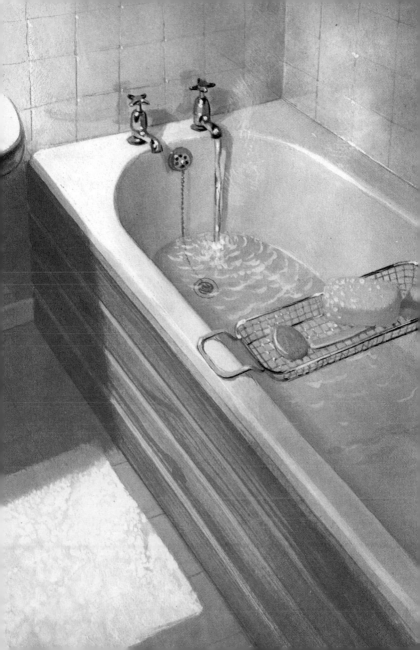

ball

Talking about a ball:

What can you do with a ball?
You can roll it, throw it, catch it in your hands, bounce it and kick it.
Shall we pretend to do all of these things?

car

Talking about a car:

Have you seen a yellow car?

cat

Talking about a cat:

Isn't this a pretty cat? Its fur is white, black and brown.
Can you point to its whiskers?

spoon

Talking about a spoon:

This is a small spoon. Do you eat your pudding with a small spoon?
What does Mother use a large spoon for?

cup

Talking about a cup:

Can you tell Mother what the letters are round this cup?

It is an empty cup. What would you like it to be filled with?

orange

Talking about an orange:

Do you like to eat sweet, juicy oranges?
Can you take the peel off by yourself?

doll

Talking about a doll:

What a pretty doll! She has long plaits of hair.
What do you think this doll's name is?

24

tap

Talking about a tap:

Can you turn a tap on and off?
The water is running from this tap, so someone must have turned it on. I wonder if it is hot or cold water.

banana

Talking about a banana:

The peel on this banana is yellow.
The peel on the orange wasn't yellow was it?
What colour was that?

brush and comb

Talking about a brush and comb:

Have you a brush and comb of your own?
Are they like those in the picture?

dog

Talking about a dog:

The dog in this picture has long ears and short legs. Have you seen a dog like this?
Perhaps it would let you stroke its long, soft ears. Let's pretend to do that.

stairs

Talking about the stairs:

I think some boys and girls have climbed up these stairs to bed, don't you?

watch

Talking about a watch:

This is a wrist watch to wear on the wrist. Where are your wrists?

Can you point to the hands on this watch, and point to the numbers?

apple

Talking about an apple:

Would you like to eat this red and green apple?
What would you do with the pips?
Some apples are yellow aren't they?

cot

Talking about a cot:

Someone has been sleeping in this cot. Who do you think it was?

What colour is the blanket?

chair

Talking about a chair:

Do you sit in a chair like this one to eat your dinner?

Perhaps you have a cushion on your chair.

bus

Talking about a bus:

I wonder if this red bus is going to the shops or to the seaside! It can't go anywhere just yet, the driver isn't in it!

biscuits

Talking about biscuits:

Which biscuit do you like best?
Why do you like that sort?
Are all the biscuits different or are there any that
are the same?

tricycle

Talking about a tricycle:

Can you ride a tricycle?
This is a red, white and blue one. There are two little wheels and one big wheel.
Let us point to the big wheel and then to the two little wheels.

book

Talking about a book:

Here is a book like your book.
Point to the cat on the cover of your book. There
are more cats inside your book.
Can you find them?

3. 10 net

We are all in you
and see if you car